Contents

Hardy Geraniums

DAVID HIBBERD

Cassell

The Royal Horticultural Society

THE ROYAL HORTICULTURAL SOCIETY

Cassell Educational Limited
Villiers House,
41/47 Strand,
London WC2N 5JE
for the Royal Horticultural Society

Copyright © David Hibberd 1994

First published 1994

British Library Cataloguing in Publication Data
A catalogue record for this book is available from the British Library

ISBN 0–304–32061–7

Line drawings by Mike Shoebridge
Photographs by David Hibberd

Phototypesetting by RGM Typesetting, Southport
Printed in Hong Kong by Wing King Tong Co. Ltd

Cover: A popular, tall border geranium, *G. psilostemon* is a parent of several good new hybrids.
Frontispiece: The markings on the petals of *G. pratense* 'Striatum' are infinitely variable.
Back cover: The soft, somewhat hoary appearance of *G. ibericum* var. *jubatum* sets off the large blue flowers to perfection.
    Photographs by David Hibberd

What is a Hardy Geranium?

The genus *Geranium* is a large one with over 400 published names and the species have a very wide distribution throughout the cool-temperate parts of the world. These plants are usually referred to as **hardy** geraniums, even though only a very few are not fully hardy in Britain, to distinguish them from the plants popularly, but incorrectly, known as geraniums which belong to the genus *Pelargonium*. Hardy geraniums are also known as cranesbills, referring to the shape of the fruit, to further distinguish them from pelargoniums.

While the genera *Geranium* and *Pelargonium* are related, both being members of the family Geraniaceae, they are quite distinct. True geraniums have radially symmetrical flowers with ten fertile stamens whereas species of *Pelargonium* have bilaterally symmetrical flowers with up to seven of the ten stamens fertile. Pelargoniums are mostly not hardy and occur naturally almost entirely within South Africa. In addition, the leaves of true geraniums are usually deeply divided and cut while those of most groups of pelargoniums are not. Pelargoniums also have rather thick, succulent stems, originating as they do from areas where they have to withstand summer drought, whereas geraniums have the appearance of "normal" herbaceous perennial plants.

The confusion between these two groups arose because for a relatively short time in the 18th century when pelargoniums were being introduced into horticulture, they were classified botanically in the genus *Geranium*, and were not finally recognised as a separate genus until 1789. The "wrong" name has stuck ever since, however, no doubt in part owing to the fact that geranium is easier to say than pelargonium. This continuing muddle confuses growers and purchasers of both geraniums and pelargoniums.

G. sylvaticum 'Album' with its pristine white flowers is one of the most striking spring-flowering geraniums

Geraniums as Garden Plants

Hardy geraniums are an easy-to-grow and versatile group of garden plants. They mix well with other herbaceous perennials and shrubs and their colours are easy to blend with virtually any colour scheme. Until relatively recently, only a few species and cultivars were widely grown but there has been an upsurge of interest in the group in recent years. Many new cultivars have been selected or bred and several species have been newly introduced into cultivation.

Most geraniums grow to between 9 in. (23 cm) and 24 in. (60 cm) tall and are clump-forming plants, producing a mound of leaves from which taller leafy flowering stems emerge. In some species no basal leaves are produced, all the leaves being borne on the flowering stems; these plants are more spreading in growth, but often still produce a mounded effect. Examples are G. rubifolium, G. sanguineum and G. wallichianum. Other species produce long leafy flowering stems with a trailing habit, these arising from a basal mound of leaves. Examples of this type are G. procurrens and G. traversii and hybrids involving one of these species as a parent, such as 'Ann Folkard', 'Dilys', 'Joy', 'Russell Prichard' and 'Salome'. Species from South Africa such as G. caffrum, G. incanum, G. pulchrum and G. robustum have trailing stems which usually become woody at the base.

LEAVES

Attractive foliage is one of the chief assets of geraniums and gives the plants considerable garden value even when they are not in flower. Most species lose their leaves in winter but those which are more or less evergreen include G. macrorrhizum, G. × oxonianum, G. phaeum and its relatives G. × monacense and G. reflexum, G. pulchrum, G. pyrenaicum, G. robustum, G. versicolor, G. traversii and hybrids involving the latter species.

Leaf size varies considerably, from less than 1 in. (2.5 cm) to more than 9 in. (23 cm) but in most species the largest dimension lies between 1½ in. (5 cm) and 5 in. (12.5 cm). Geranium leaves are

G. psilostemon 'Bressingham Flair' is a magnificent summer-flowering border geranium with flowers of a less intense colour than the typical form

Key to leaves

1 *swatense* **2** *sessiliflorum* subsp. *novaezelandiae* 'Nigricans'
3 *sessiflorum* subsp. *novaezelandiae* 'Porter's Pass' **4** *orientalitibeticum*
5 × *monacense* 'Muldoon' **6** *versicolor* **7** *sanguineum* 'Elsbeth' **8** *wlassovianum*
9 *renardii* **10** 'Ann Folkard' **11** *phaeum* 'Samobor' **12** 'Black Ice' **13** *argenteum*
14 'Sea Spray' **15** *macrorrhizum* 'Variegatum' **16** *yunnanense* **17** *incanum*
18 × *oxonianum* 'Walter's Gift' **19** *cinereum* subsp. *subcaulescens* **20** *clarkei*
21 *traversii* var. *elegans* **22** *soboliferum*

rounded in outline but are always split into a number of divisions, usually five, these mostly being further divided in various ways producing a dainty effect. Species in which the leaves are particularly finely dissected or sharply divided include *G. clarkei*, *G. collinum*, *G. incanum*, *G. malviflorum*, *G. pylzowianum*, *G. soboliferum*, *G. transbaicalicum*, *G. tuberosum* and *G. yesoense*. Species in which the main lobes of the leaves are not intricately divided include *G. gracile*, *G. nodosum*, *G. platyanthum*, *G. pyrenaicum*, *G. renardii*, *G. rubifolium*, *G. traversii* and *G. wlassovianum*.

The leaves of many geraniums are coloured or marked in ways which give them additional interest. Some, including *G. argenteum*, *G. cinereum*, *G. incanum*, *G. pulchrum*, *G. renardii*, *G. robust-*

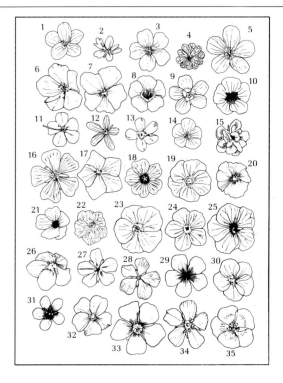

Key to flowers

1 *palustre* **2** × *oxonianum* 'Southcombe Double' **3** × *oxonianum* 'A. T. Johnson'
4 *versicolor* **5** 'Nimbus' **6** 'Spinners' **7** *pratense* 'Striatum'
8 *cinereum* subsp. *subcaulescens* 'Splendens' **9** *caffrum* **10** 'Ann Folkard'
11 *cantabrigiense* 'Cambridge' **12** *asphodeloides* 'Prince Regent'
13 *sylvaticum* 'Mayflower' **14** 'Mavis Simpson' **15** *pratense* 'Plenum
Violaceum' **16** *renardii* **17** 'Brookside' **18** *cinereum* 'Ballerina' **19** *rubifolium*
20 *sanguineum* 'Striatum' **21** *cinereum* subsp. *subcaulescens*
22 × *oxonianum* 'Hollywood' **23** *himalayense* **24** *erianthum* 'Calm Sea'
25 *psilostemon* 'Bressingham Flair' **26** 'Blue Pearl' **27** 'Pagoda' **28** *shikokianum*
29 *maderense* **30** *swatense* **31** *procurrens* **32** 'Russell Prichard'
33 *lambertii* 'Swansdown' **34** *maculatum* **35** *wallichianum* 'Buxton's Variety'

um and *G. traversii* have greyish or silvery leaves; *G. monacense*
'Muldoon', *G. phaeum* and *G. versicolor* have chocolate-brown
blotches between the leaf divisions; *G. lambertii*, *G. orientalitibeticum*, *G. pogonanthum*, *G. sinense* and *G. wallichianum* have leaves
mottled in more than one shade of green giving a marbled
appearance; and *G. sessiliflorum* subsp. *novaezelandiae* 'Nigricans'
and its hybrids have bronze-tinted leaves. Only a very few

geraniums have variegated leaves, the most noteworthy being *G. macrorrhizum* 'Variegatum' and *G. phaeum* 'Variegatum'.

FLOWERS

Size and shape
Geranium flowers are uniform and simple in structure having five sepals, five petals, ten stamens and five carpels (female parts), these elements being symmetrically arranged. The flowers are usually bowl shaped or funnel shaped and the petals may be broad and overlapping or narrower with spaces between them. The flowers of most species and cultivars are between ¾ in. (2 cm) and 1½ in. (4 cm) in diameter. Species with relatively small flowers borne in quantity may create just as great an effect as species producing smaller numbers of much larger flowers.

Flowering time
Length of flowering time and season of flowering vary considerably between species. In general, summer-dormant species start to flower in early spring together with the earliest of those which begin to flower before midsummer. Most geraniums flower between late spring and midsummer and if clump-forming species are cut hard back after the main flush of flowers they will produce a

A hybrid between *G. psilostemon* and *G. procurrens*, 'Anne Thomson' produces its strongly coloured flowers continuously from early summer to autumn

new leaf-mound and in most cases a second flush of flowers. Geraniums flowering after midsummer include most of the species originating from eastern Asia; hybrids inheriting their late-flowering from one of their parents; and sterile hybrids which have a long season of flowering extending on both sides of midsummer which may or may not have a late-flowering parent. It is important to note that not all sterile hybrids flower recurrently (e.g. G. × magnificum) and not all recurrently-flowering hybrids are sterile (e.g. G. × oxonianum).

Colour

Geranium flowers range in colour between pink and violet-blue; there is no true blue geranium, even the bluest containing some red. Most of the pinks and reds are also tinged with blue but a few cultivars including one of the most widely grown, G. × oxonianum 'Wargrave Pink' have salmon-pink flowers. About one-sixth of the geraniums included here have white or nearly white flowers. Excluding those with small flowers and forms with veined petals, the following are particularly effective for their pure white flowers: G. asphodeloides 'Starlight', G. maculatum 'Album', G. phaeum 'Album', G. pratense 'Galactic', G. sanguineum 'Album' and G. sylvaticum 'Album'.

The colour range in Geranium is especially difficult to describe

The flowers of G. oxonianum 'Winscombe' change in colour from almost white to purplish pink as they age. It is one of the smaller of the many cultivars of this hybrid species

G. wallichianum 'Syabru' is a cultivar of wild origin with reddish purple flowers

and the solution adopted here is to divide it into six colour groups for which a representative selection of species is given in the following table. Species and cultivars are listed in order of increasing blue content.

SALMON PINK
oxonianum 'Southcombe
  Double'
oxonianum 'Wargrave Pink'
oxonianum 'Wageningen'

PALE AND DEEP PINK
oxonianum 'Winscombe'
oxonianum 'Walters Gift'
cinereum subsp. *subcaulescens*
  'Splendens'
sanguineum 'Jubilee Pink'
sanguineum 'Shepherd's
  Warning'

PURPLISH RED AND PINK
endressii

'Mavis Simpson'
reflexum
'Sea Fire'
oxonianum 'Phoebe Noble'
oxonianum 'Rosenlicht'

REDDISH-PURPLE
cinereum subcaulescens
'Patricia'
psilostemon
macrorrhizum 'Bevan's
  Variety'
'Russell Prichard'
palmatum
nervosum
sanguineum 'Elsbeth'
wallichianum 'Syabru'

'Spinners' has the most richly coloured flowers of all the hybrids of G. *pratense*

oxonianum 'Miriam Rundle'
brutium
gracile
oxonianum 'Claridge Druce'
collinum
orientalitibeticum
rubifolium
'Ann Folkard'
cantabrigiense 'Cambridge'
albanum
fremontii
swatense
'Dilys'

BLUISH-PURPLE
phaeum 'Joan Baker'
pulchrum
robustum
wlassovianum
himalayense 'Plenum'
incanum
clarkei 'Kashmir Purple'

sylvaticum 'Silva'
platyanthum
'Nimbus'
'Philippe Vapelle'
magnificum
'Spinners'
sylvaticum 'Mayflower'

VIOLET-BLUE
bohemicum
pratense 'Mrs Kendall Clark'
erianthum 'Neptune'
'Blue Pearl'
regelii
'Brookside'
himalayense 'Irish Blue'
himalayense 'Gravetye'
'Johnson's Blue'
pratense 'Striatum'
pratense 'Plenum Caeruleum'
sylvaticum 'Amy Doncaster'
wallichianum 'Buxton's Variety'

Where to Grow Geraniums

The vast majority of geraniums are completely hardy in Britain and are easy to grow in any garden soil, either acid or alkaline. They are not particularly susceptible to pests and diseases. Most will grow in conditions of full sun to half shade, and the majority are also drought tolerant; a few are even drought resistant making them valuable plants for dry shade. This wide range of tolerance, together with the fact that many geraniums are free to increase and easy to divide makes them ideal ground cover plants, probably the best of all genera of herbaceous plants for this purpose.

A few species, mainly those from eastern Asia including *G. erianthum*, *G. lambertii*, *G. polyanthes*, *G. pogonanthum*, *G. shikokianum*, *G. sinense*, *G. soboliferum*, *G. wallichianum* and *G. yunnanense*, are more demanding. They seem to need a soil that does not dry out in summer and a moist atmosphere. In the south and east of England, where the air is dry and light values are high in summer, these species seem to grow best in part shade.

A small number of geraniums are not fully hardy. Most notable among these are three species native to the Canary Islands or Madeira, *G. canariense*, *G. maderense* and *G. palmatum*. All are large and imposing plants, however, and well worth any extra effort involved in providing the right winter conditions. *G. palmatum* is the hardiest of the three, surviving most winters in the south and west of England in a sheltered part of the garden. In other parts of Britain it is worth overwintering plants in pots in a cold greenhouse and planting these out in spring for the summer display of flowers. This strategy cannot be applied to *G. maderense* and *G. canariense*, however, since they produce massive leaf rosettes during the autumn and winter, and their inflorescences from spring onwards. Ideal growing conditions are provided by a frost-free greenhouse. *G. maderense* usually dies after flowering but is easily and quickly grown again from seed.

Geranium traversii and *G. incanum* are often lost in winter but both are easily raised from seed, the latter also from cuttings.

Above: G. pogonanthum produces its delicate and beautifully constructed nodding pink flowers in late summer
Below: G. sanguineum 'Glenluce', one of the larger cultivars of the species, has particularly pale flowers and silky leaves

Propagation

DIVISION

The majority of geraniums are easy to propagate by division of the rootstock and even though most forms are long-lasting and need little attention in the garden, plants can be rejuvenated with advantage every few years by lifting clumps, enriching the soil and replanting healthy divisions. The easiest species to increase in this way are those with a fibrous root system such as *G. × oxonianum*; those with a surface mat of rhizomes such as *G. × cantabrigiense*, *G. dalmaticum*, *G. endressii*, *G. macrorrhizum* and *G. phaeum*; and those spreading by underground rhizomes such as *G. clarkei*, *G. himalayense* and *G. kishtvariense*. Clumps of these species may be pulled or prised apart in the autumn or in spring when growth is just starting. Autumn divisions have the advantage that they will have a chance to grow new roots in moist and still relatively warm soil, and so will better withstand any following spring drought; divisions made in spring may need watering until established. Large clumps may be divided into a few pieces or they may be pulled apart into plantlets consisting of a small piece of the rootstock and stem or a piece of rhizome, and a tuft of leaves. Such divisions are best potted up and grown on until established before replanting. This method of working has the advantage that the plants may be divided in August, after the main flush of flowers. The small potted divisions will be ready for planting out in late autumn, and it is possible in this way quickly to produce substantial areas of ground cover of species such as *G. macrorrhizum*, *G. endressii*, *G. × oxonianum* and *G. phaeum*.

Some geraniums such as *G. pratense* and *G. psilostemon* have a compact rootstock, with a more or less permanent underground stem. These should be divided as growth begins in spring since autumn divisions frequently die in winter. The divisions are grown on preferably in a pot until large enough for planting in late spring.

Other species with compact rootstocks such as *G. wallichianum* and *G. oreganum* are difficult to divide, as they have only a few long thick roots and a small number of growing points. Although they

The pale flowers of *G. phaeum* var. *lividum* 'Joan Baker' appear luminous in woodland shade

can be divided with care in spring, only a small number of new plants will be produced and the divisions will need to be potted up and grown on. Plants of this type are best propagated by seed, and this is the reason why certain cultivars such as *G. wallichianum* 'Buxton's Variety' are not clonal (propagated vegetatively from a single plant and therefore genetically identical).

Summer-dormant species such as *G. libani* and *G. tuberosum* are most easily increased by division at any time during the dormant season, though with *G. macrostylum* and *G. malviflorum* it may be necessary to wait until leaves appear in autumn to establish the location of their small tubers. *G. orientalitibeticum* and *G. pylzowianum* also have small tubers and these can be separated either during the dormant period, if they can be found, or in spring as the leaves begin to grow.

CUTTINGS

Cuttings are not widely used in propagating geraniums since the above-ground stems of most species are inflorescences and will not root. In some species, however, such as *G. incanum*, *G. sanguineum* and *G. wallichianum*, there is no basal rosette of leaves as all of the

The white flowers of *G. macrorrhizum* 'Album' contrast well with the dark evergreen leaves

leaves are borne on flowering stems. Cuttings of these leafy stems can often be rooted, but success will depend on the condition of the material, vigorously-growing shoots being preferable to weaker growth. The trailing flowering stems of G. *traversii* and its hybrids can also be used for cuttings.

The long rhizomes of G. *sanguineum* can be cut into pieces about $1\frac{1}{2}$ in. (4 cm) long and treated as root-cuttings by burying them horizontally about $\frac{3}{4}$ in. (2 cm) deep in cutting compost; they will produce new shoots and roots in about eight weeks.

G. *argenteum* and G. *cinereum*, and hybrids between them, referred to as G. × *lindavicum*, are particularly difficult to divide. This is because they have a compact root system consisting of a mass of fibrous roots from which arises a thick underground stem dividing just above ground level into a crown of semi-woody branches from the tips of which the leaves grow. These species are best propagated by stem cuttings, each consisting of one of the ultimate divisions taken from the crown of the plant. The cuttings can be severed from the plant with a very sharp blade at any time from when growth starts in early spring until summer; early cuttings will have the longest time to make a plant large enough to survive the following winter. The cuttings should be prepared by

G. *lindavicum* 'Apple Blossom' is a less-common rock garden geranium, well worth searching out for its pretty pale pink flowers and silvery leaves

removing all the old leaf remains and all the leaves except the very youngest ones at the tip.

These cuttings root in a wide range of media and in a variety of conditions, but use of an open-structured compost and treatment with hormone rooting powder, which consists largely of a fungicide base, are obvious recommendations. Any method which has proved reliable for rooting cuttings of other herbaceous material should also work for cuttings of this type.

Geranium procurrens is exceptional among geraniums in having long flowering stems that root at the leaf joints where they touch the ground in the same way as strawberry runners. It is therefore very easy to propagate by nodal cuttings. Its hybrids 'Ann Folkard', 'Anne Thomson' and 'Salome' do not root naturally in this way, but stem cuttings can be rooted. Since these cultivars have very long internodes they are best rooted at a leaf-bearing node. The cuttings must be inserted shallowly to avoid burying the base of the leaf stem, or petiole, and a short piece of stem should be left below the node to keep the cutting stable in the compost. Cuttings of this type should be taken as early as possible in order to produce a plant with leaves growing from an underground stem by the end of the season.

SEED

In general geraniums are easy to grow from seed. However, since most forms are so easy to divide, seed is best used to increase those that are difficult or slow to propagate vegetatively.

Gathering seed

It is important to realise the seed dispersal mechanism in geraniums is explosive, and therefore seed must be gathered when ripe but before it is dispersed.

After geranium flowers are fertilised, the petals fall and the base of the style rapidly lengthens and thickens to form a structure known as the rostrum, the "cranesbill". At the base of the rostrum are five fruit segments, the mericarps, each containing one seed. As the rostrum matures it usually turns brown as it gradually dries out. Eventually five strips of the rostrum, the awns, each attached to one mericarp, spring violently away from a central column flinging away the seeds. The critical stage for collection, when the seeds are ripe but before they have been ejected, can be recognised by the darkening of the rostrum and the slight lifting away of the mericarps from the central column. Sufficient seed can usually be

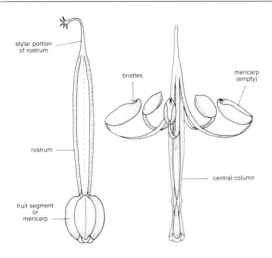

The parts of the fruit of Geranium: left, when nearly mature; right, after discharge

obtained by visiting, every two to four days, plants which are setting seed since the flowers are not all produced together and fruits may be found at various stages of development.

In the majority of geranium species the empty carpels remain attached to the end of the central column by their awns after discharge, producing a candelabrum-like structure. Since the seed dispersal mechanism is highly efficient it is useless searching these structures for remaining seed. It is, on the other hand, useful to know that some species vary from this typical pattern, the awns becoming detached at discharge leaving a bare central column. No candelabrum-like structure is therefore produced, and there is thus no obvious indication that mature seed has been produced and that more will follow from later-developing fruits. Species which disperse their seed in this way include G. albanum, G. argenteum, G. aristatum, G. bohemicum, G. brutium, G. canariense, G. cataractarum, G. cinereum, G. dalmaticum, G. gracile, G. ibericum, G. libani, G. × lindavicum, G. macrorrhizum, G. macrostylum, G. maderense, G. malviflorum, G. × monacense, G. palmatum, G. phaeum, G. platypetalum, G. polyanthes, G. pyrenaicum, G. reflexum, G. renardii, G. robertianum, G. rubescens and G. tuberosum.

Sowing and growing
Seed is best sown in spring. When sown in autumn, the seedlings that are produced immediately are vulnerable to winter growing

conditions and, in any case, most seed usually germinates in spring. Most seed composts, including soil-less types, are suitable for spring sowing, though if sporadic or delayed germination is found to occur for a particular species then a loam-based compost may be preferred since this is much less likely to dry out. The seed should be spaced individually on the firmed surface of the compost and covered with a thin layer of horticultural vermiculite or sieved compost if a soil-less type is used, or with about $\frac{1}{4}$ in. (5 mm) of grit for a soil-based compost. The pots are watered from below by standing them in a deep waterbath until moisture appears at the surface. The pots should be covered with glass and placed in a frame or sheltered place until the seeds germinate, usually within a few weeks. The glass should then be removed and the pots of seedlings placed in good light but shaded from direct sunlight which can scorch the leaves. The seedlings are pricked out when the first true leaves have developed.

Seedlings of most species grow fast and are best grown in individual pots of $\frac{1}{3}$ or $\frac{1}{2}$ litre volume (approximately 3 inches and 4 inches in diameter). The young plants may be planted out as soon as they have made a good root system; this will usually be in early summer for seed sown in early spring. Most species flower in the year following germination but some take longer and most species will, in any case, take two to three years to grow to their normal size and attain their typical habit of growth.

All forms of G. *asphodeloides* subsp. *asphodeloides* produce large numbers of small starry flowers on spreading growth

Hybrids and Hybridisation

A number of well-known geraniums including 'A. T. Johnson', 'Johnson's Blue', G. x *magnificum* and 'Russell Prichard' are of hybrid origin but many other hybrids are now available. Some of these have arisen in gardens, including botanic gardens, as chance seedlings or have been raised from open-pollinated seed. Cultivars of this type include: 'Ann Folkard', 'Brookside', 'Kate', G. x *monacense*, 'Nimbus', G. x *oxonianum* (many cultivars), 'Salome', 'Spinners' and 'Stanhoe'. Other cultivars have resulted from deliberate hybridisation, either with the aim of producing attractive garden plants such as the G. *cinereum* hybrids 'Apple Blossom', 'Ballerina' and 'Lawrence Flatman', or as a result of scientific research, such as G. x *cantabrigiense* 'Cambridge'. Recently, a number of hybrids of horticultural value have been produced as a result of a major hybridisation programme by Alan Bremner working in the Orkney Islands. Cultivars named so far include: 'Anne Thomson', 'Black Ice', 'Chantilly', 'Dilys', 'Joy', 'Little Gem', 'Nora Bremner', 'Pagoda', 'Patricia', 'Rebecca', 'Sea Pink', 'Sea Spray', 'Sea Fire' and 'St. Ola'.

Some species cross so easily that wherever they grow in

'Joy' inherits its spreading habit and long flowering season from G. *traversii* var. *elegans* and its marbled leaves from G. *lambertii*

proximity, hybrid seedlings may be expected. For example, the New Zealand species *G. traversii* and *G. sessiliflorum* readily hybridise and each of them crosses with the European species *G. endressii*, and with *G. × oxonianum*, itself a hybrid between *G. endressii* and *G. versicolor*. If parental species like these are grown together, eventually a garden may contain a "hybrid swarm" – a range of plants produced by repeated crossing and back crossing. Other examples of species that hybridise easily are *G. argenteum × G. cinereum* (= *G. × lindavicum*) and *G. phaeum × G. reflexum* (= *G. × monacense*). Similarly, the various colour forms and geographical variants of *G. pratense* hybridise readily with each other and with closely-related species such as *G. clarkei* and *G. collinum*.

HOW TO HYBRIDISE

Hybridising geraniums is not a particularly difficult process, but the chance of producing a new garden-worthy plant is so small that it is important to choose the most promising parents. Species which have proved particularly valuable include *G. lambertii*, *G. psilostemon*, *G. wallichianum* 'Buxton's Variety', *G. traversii* and *G. sessiliflorum*.

Controlled hybridisation is best carried out using pot-grown plants in the protection of a greenhouse. Most geraniums will grow tall with rather soft growth under protection and will need to be supported. The flowers have distinct male and female stages, the anthers releasing pollen before the stigmas curl back and are ready to receive pollen. The anthers should therefore be removed with fine forceps or scissors just before or soon after the flower opens.

The emasculated flowers are then protected from insect pollination by using translucent bags closed around the flower stem by means of a paperclip. When the stigmas spread, usually about two days after bud-burst, they are fertilised by touching them with a pollen-producing anther from the male parent. The flower of the pollen parent should also, preferably, have been bagged before opening to prevent any possible contamination with pollen from another species by visiting bees. The bag is then replaced over the pollinated flower both to continue to protect it against cross-pollination and to retain the ripe seeds. (Unsuccessful pollination will result in a withered flower.) The name of the pollen parent should be written on the bag before it is replaced after pollination, and both parents carefully recorded on the seed packet when the seed is gathered.

Above: The lovely flowers of 'Nora Bremner' are intermediate between those of its parents *G. rubifolium* and *G. wallichianum* 'Buxton's Variety' and are produced from midsummer onwards
Below: The flowers of *G. wallichianum* 'Buxton's Variety' are at their best in the cooler weather of early autumn

An A to Z of Geraniums

This listing includes the great majority of species presently in cultivation. In the case of species which have a large number of cultivars, a selection of the most distinctive is given.

Heights are not given unless the plants are taller than 24 in. (60 cm) when they are referred to as large, or grow to between about 5 in. (13 cm) and 9 in. (23 cm) when they are termed small.

Flower size is not given unless the flowers are less than $\frac{3}{4}$ in. (2 cm) across – small, or exceed $1\frac{1}{2}$ in. (4 cm) – large.

Leaf size is not given unless the leaves are less than $1\frac{1}{2}$ in. (4 cm) across – small, or greater than 5 in. (13 cm) across – large.

Flowering times are approximate and the start of flowering will vary with the earliness or lateness of the season, the latitude and the aspect of the garden. Later-flowering forms will also continue to flower longer in a mild autumn.

✱ This indicates species and cultivars considered to be of particular garden merit.
𝄞 This indicates plants with particularly striking leaves.
   Suitable garden uses and the best method of propagation are given at the end of the entry for each species or cultivar.

G. albanum
A dome of leaves and wiry trailing flower stems each up to 4 ft (1.2 m) long. Flowers pale reddish purple with a pale centre and strongly veined petals. May to June. Dormant in midsummer. Border; large rock garden. Seed; division in spring.

G. albiflorum
Sprays of small white flowers on erect stems in May and June and then recurrently. Wild/woodland garden. Division; seed.

'Patricia', a hybrid between G. psilostemon and G. endressii, produces its strongly coloured dark-eyed flowers continuously from June to September

29

G. anemonifolium see G. palmatum

*G. 'Ann Folkard' (procurrens × psilostemon)
A magnificent geranium producing a mound of golden green leaves in early spring followed by long leafy flowering stems. Flowers large, strong reddish purple with a dark centre and dark veins. Summer to autumn. Large border. Division in spring.

*G. 'Anne Thomson' (procurrens × psilostemon)
Similar to 'Anne Folkard' but growing to only about half the size.

*G. argenteum
Small and compact mounds of round deeply divided, silvery leaves set off the relatively large flowers which vary from almost white to pale reddish purple in different clones. A truly alpine geranium needing full sun, perfect drainage and protection from winter wet. June and July. Rock garden/alpine house. Cuttings in spring; seed.

G. aristatum
A hairy sprawling and untidy plant, having curious nodding flowers with strongly reflexed petals. Petals almost white, strongly veined with purple. May, recurrent through summer. Wild/woodland garden. Division; seed difficult to germinate.

G. asphodeloides
Densely leafy, mounding plants producing large numbers of starry flowers recurrently from May onwards. Flower colour variable. Border, large rock garden. Division; seed.
    G. asphodeloides subsp. asphodeloides. Flowers mid purplish pink or white.
    'Prince Regent'. Pale purplish pink petals with five fine dark veins.
    G. asphodeloides subsp. crenophilum. The petals are broader than in subsp. asphodeloides, always deep pink.
    G. 'Starlight' (subsp. asphodeloides × subsp. crenophilum). Pure white flowers with broader petals than in 'Prince Regent'.

G. atlanticum see G. malviflorum

G. 'Black Ice' (selected seedling from sessiliflorum subsp. novaezelandiae 'Nigricans' × traversii var. elegans)
Mounds of dark bronze shiny leaves and sprawling leafy flowering stems up to 3 ft (90 cm) long. Flowers small, white. The dark colour

Left: Although of rather lax growth G. *aristatum* is cultivated for its curious cyclamen-like flowers
Right: G. *phaeum* 'Rose Madder' has brownish pink flowers, a colour not found in other geraniums

of the foliage does not show up well against soil but would contrast spreading over pale paving or trailing over a stone wall. Recurrent from May. Division.

G. 'Blue Pearl' (selected seedling from 'Brookside')
Loosely mounding plants, flowers bowl shaped, pale violet-blue with darker veins. May to June. Border. Division.

G. *bohemicum*
A biennial with rather untidy growth but its violet-blue flowers merit a place in the woodland/wild garden. Recurrent. Seed.

∗G. 'Brookside' (*clarkei* 'Kashmir Purple' × *pratense*)
Finely divided leaves and bowl shaped, violet-blue flowers with a pale centre. May to mid-July. Border. Division.

G. *brutium*
Showy annual with rounded, bluntly lobed leaves and bright reddish purple flowers. March onwards, from overwintered seedlings. Rock garden; wild garden. Seed, self-sowing.

G. *brycei*
Sub-shrubby trailing stems form large leafy mounds. Flowers bluish purple. A recently introduced species from South Africa, hardy in normal winters. June to July. Border; wild garden. Seed.

G. 'Buxton's Variety' see *G. wallichianum* 'Buxton's Variety'

G. caeruleatum (= *G. sylvaticum* subsp. *caeruleatum*)
Mounds of small leaves only a few inches tall covered in small violet-blue flowers in May. Rock garden. Division in spring.

G. caffrum
A hardy South African species with sub-shrubby, sprawling stems, eventually mounding, and evergreen leaves. Flowers light reddish purple, white centred, freely produced in June. Border; wild garden. Seed.

∗G. canariense
A rosette of very large, aromatic, shiny, deeply lobed leaves grows during the autumn and winter. Flowers from April to July in a spectacular inflorescence. Petals reddish ˙purple on the upper surface and very pale, almost white, underneath. Not hardy; cold greenhouse. Seed.

∗G. cantabrigiense (*dalmaticum* × *macrorrhizum*)
A good ground-cover plant with shiny, aromatic evergreen leaves, tolerant of a wide range of growing conditions. Spring and early summer. Border; rock garden. Division.
  'Biokovo'. Low spreading habit and white flowers which are almost always pink-stained and veined.
  ∗'Cambridge'. The most vigorous cultivar with reddish purple flowers.
  'Karmina'. Very similar to 'Cambridge'.
  ∗'St. Ola' (*dalmaticum* 'Album' × *macrorrhizum* 'Album'). Similar to 'Biokovo' but differs in having whiter flowers, rarely showing any pink; broader, flatter petals, and deeper green leaves.

G. cataractarum
A small and attractive, rather short-lived species with a brittle texture. Leaves evergreen, small and delicately divided. Flowers small, funnel-shaped, bright reddish purple with an eye of orange anthers. Prefers some shade and resents drying out. Recurrent from May. Rock garden. Seed.
  Subsp. pitardii. Narrower petals than subsp. *cataractarum*, these fading to white at the base.

G. 'Chantilly' (*gracile* × *renardii*)
A recent hybrid inheriting the upright habit of *G. gracile* and with

similar but larger pale reddish purple flowers, held above the foliage. Leaves pale green, similar in shape to those of *G. gracile*, but with the surface wrinkled as in *G. renardii*. May to June. Border. Division.

∗G. cinereum

A very variable alpine species closely related to *G. argenteum* though generally less demanding. Some of the named forms are among the best known small geraniums. Spring and early summer. Rock garden. Cuttings in spring; root cuttings.

Subsp. cinereum var. cinereum (= *cinereum* var. *cinereum*) has white or pink flowers and the leaves are more deeply and sharply divided than in other varieties.

'Album' (= *cinereum* var. *cinereum* 'Album'; *cinereum* var. *album*). Completely white flowers.

Subsp. subcaulescens var. obtusilobum (= *cinereum* var. *obtusilobum*). Pale green, rounded, bluntly lobed leaves which are smaller than those in other varieties. Flowers bowl shaped, very pale pink and delicately veined. Charming and desirable but scarce.

Var. subcaulescens (= *cinereum* var. *subcaulescens*). One of the most strikingly coloured of all geraniums having bright reddish purple flowers with a very dark centre.

Var. subcaulescens 'Giuseppii' (= *cinereum* var. *subcaulescens* 'Giuseppii'; *cinereum* subsp. *subcaulescens* forma *giuseppii*). The flowers are less stridently coloured than in var. *subcaulescens* and the centre is less dark and less concentrated. The name is usually misspelled 'Guiseppii'.

Var. subcaulesens 'Splendens' (= *cinereum* var. *subcaulescens* 'Splendens'; *cinereum* subsp. *subcaulescens* forma *splendens*). Bright pink flowers with a dark centre. Petals broad, producing flatter flowers with a more circular outline than in other forms of var. *subcaulescens*.

HYBRID CULTIVARS

'Ballerina' (*cinereum* subsp. *cinereum* × *cinereum* subsp. *subcaulescens*). Pale reddish purple flowers with a dark reddish purple centre and the petals are heavily and finely veined.

'Lawrence Flatman' (*cinereum* subsp. *cinereum* × *cinereum* subsp. *subcaulesens*). Very similar to 'Ballerina' but the petals have an elongated triangle of darker ground colour in the middle of the petals, its tip pointing towards the base.

∗ G. clarkei
Leaves deeply and finely cut. Habit of growth similar to that of
G. pratense, but plants smaller. Flower colour variable. Spring and
early summer. Border. Division.
   'Kashmir Pink'. A seedling from 'Kashmir Purple' with pale
pink flowers.
   'Kashmir Purple' (= pratense 'Kashmir Purple'; bergianum and
'bergerianum' [misapplied]). Bluish purple flowers with a pale eye.
   'Kashmir White' (= pratense 'Kashmir White'; rectum album
[misapplied]). White flowers with fine pink veins. Less free to
increase than the above two cultivars.

G. collinum
Growth rather loose, leaves deeply and finely cut. Flowers pale
reddish purple from June to September. Woodland/wild garden.
Division; seed.

∗ G. 'Coombeland White' (lambertii × traversii)
Similar to 'Joy' but with white to very pale pink flowers with pink
veins.

G. dahuricum
A delicate sprawling plant very similar to G. yesoense with small
deeply and sharply cut leaves and pale bluish purple flowers from
June to August. Rock garden; border. Seed; division.

G. dalmaticum
Plants small, with creeping rhizomes and small, glossy, scented
evergreen leaves. Flowers pale reddish purple with a distinctly
inflated calyx. An easy rock garden plant thriving in poor gritty
soil. Spring and early summer. Division.
   'Album' (= dalmaticum var. album). Flowers white.

G. 'Dilys' (procurrens × sanguineum)
A recent hybrid producing long, widely spreading and mounding
leafy stems bearing dark green leaves similar to those of
G. sanguineum. Flowers reddish purple with a dark centre and
veined petals freely produced from August to October. Border;
large rock garden. Division; cuttings.

∗ G. endressii
A mounding, ground covering, almost evergreen species with
bright purplish pink flowers from May to September. Many plants

G. cinereum 'Ballerina' is one of the best known of all geraniums, an easy and reliable cultivar for the rock garden and other freely drained places

sold as G. endressii or G. endressii hybrids should be classified as G. × oxonianum. G. endressii is distinguished by the fact that its early growth produces a low even carpet of leaves while G. × oxonianum cultivars make mounds of leaves. G. endressii leaves are never brown-blotched while those of G. × oxonianum have brown markings (sometimes clearly visible only occasionally) at the bases of the leaf divisions, a character inherited from its other parent, G. versicolor. Ground cover; border; woodland/wild garden. Division.

'Rosenlicht' see G. × oxonianum 'Rosenlicht'
'Wageningen' see G. × oxonianum 'Wageningen'
'Wargrave Pink' see G. × oxonianum 'Wargrave Pink'

✳ G. erianthum

Sprays of usually pale violet-blue flowers with delicate petals are produced recurrently from May onwards. A lovely woodland plant, the flowers having particular luminosity in shade. Division (cultivars); seed.

'Calm Sea'. A tall cultivar with flowers of palest blue with strong, very dark blue feathery veining.

'Neptune'. Large deep blue flowers, and a more spreading habit than other forms.

'**Undine**' (= *erianthum album*). Pure white flowers with yellow anthers and a low habit of growth.

G. *eriostemon* see G. *platyanthum*

*G. *farreri*
A dwarf alpine species with small, round, bluntly lobed, faintly marbled leaves. Flowers large relative to the size of the plant, very pale pink with dark anthers. A much coveted plant, and certainly the most desirable of the alpine geraniums. This is a scree plant in nature and a perfectly drained gritty soil in sun is essential. May to June. Seed.

G. *flanaganii*
Sprawling sub-shrubby stems ultimately producing leafy mounds. A South African species very similar to G. *caffrum* but the flowers have pink prominently veined petals. June. Wild garden. Seed.

G. *fremontii*
Much-branched flowering stems covered in sticky hairs produce clusters of upward-facing, pale reddish purple flowers recurrently from May to August. Wild/woodland garden. Seed.

*G. *gracile*
Tall elegant plants, essential for any woodland garden. Leaves light green with five sharply pointed divisions which are not divided

The beautifully veined, pale blue flowers of G. *erianthum* 'Calm Sea' are at their best in woodland shade

further. Flowers funnel-shaped with narrow petals, each with three to five short dark narrow veins in the lower half. May onwards. Division; seed.
'Blanche'. Flowers pale pink.
'Blush'. The best known form with purplish pink flowers.

G. grandiflorum see **G. himalayense**

G. grevilleanum see **G. lambertii**

✳ G. himalayense (= G. grandiflorum)
Handsome leaves and large, violet-blue, shallowly bowl-shaped flowers from April to July. The flowers are flushed reddish purple in the centre. Ground cover, in any garden habitat. Division.
'Baby Blue'. Plants compact, growing to only 12 in. (30 cm) tall. Flowers very large, similar to those of 'Gravetye' but borne more freely.
'Gravetye' (= G. grandiflorum var. alpinum [misapplied]). Extra large flowers with the central purplish flush particularly prominent.
'Irish Blue'. The lovely pale blue flowers have an even larger central purplish area than 'Gravetye'.
'Plenum' (= 'Birch Double'). Smaller than the other cultivars, with smaller more rounded leaves. Flowers double, bluish purple. Often sold erroneously as G. pratense 'Plenum Violaceum'.

✳ G. ibericum
Var. ibericum. Large hairy plants with large, divided leaves. The large, dark-veined, violet-blue flowers are produced abundantly in June. Plants sold under this name are usually found to be the hybrid species G. × magnificum which it closely resembles and of which it is a parent. Border. Division; seed.
Var. jubatum. The flowers are smaller, bluer and more heavily veined, and the whole plant is more noticeably hairy than var. ibericum giving a hoary greyish appearance.

✳ ⚘ G. incanum var. multifidum
Sprawling habit, very finely divided leaves, dark green above, whitish below. Flowers a strong bluish purple, recurrent from May. Rock garden; border. Not very hardy but comes true from seed and stem cuttings root easily.

✳ G. 'Ivan'
Like a small G. psilostemon with reddish purple, dark centred

flowers. 8 in. (25 cm) tall. June to September. Border. Division.

*G. 'Johnson's Blue' (*himalayense* × *pratense*)
An old but still very popular hybrid. Loose mounds of deeply and sharply divided leaves bear violet-blue flowers from late May through summer. Border. Division.

*G. 'Joy' (*traversii* var. *elegans* × *lambertii*)
Mounds of evergreen marbled leaves and pale reddish purple flowers with a dark centre and prominent veining from June to September. An excellent new plant for the large rock garden or front of the border. Division in spring; cuttings.

*G. 'Kashmir Blue'
(*clarkei* 'Kashmir White' × *pratense albiflorum*)
Large plants similar to G. *pratense*. Flowers large, pale violet-blue in colour. Late May to July. Plants of G. *clarkei* closely resembling, but not identical to, G. *clarkei* 'Kashmir Purple' are sometimes sold under this name. Border. Division in spring.

G. 'Kate'
(*endressii* × *sessiliflorum* subsp. *novaezelandiae* 'Nigricans')
Small trailing plants with bronzy leaves and small pale-pink flowers with dark veins from May to September. Rock garden. Division in spring; cuttings.

*G. kishtvariense
Large reddish purple flowers with a white centre and veined petals are held well above a mound of sharply lobed leaves. Part shade and in soil that does not dry out in summer. June to September. Division; seed.

G. lambertii (= G. *grevilleanum*)
A species with a sprawling habit best grown through other plants. Finely marbled leaves and large nodding pale pink or white flowers with a purplish red centre and veined petals. July to August. Woodland; large rock garden in soil that does not dry out in summer. Seed; cuttings; careful division in spring.
  'Swansdown' (= G. *candidum* [misapplied]). The name given to the white-flowered, red-centred form.

*G. libani
Dormant through the hottest months, produces fresh leaves in

Left: The jewel-like flowers of aptly named 'Little Gem' are borne from May to October on wide-spreading, leafy stems
Right: One of the best known of all geraniums, G. × *magnificum* produces its stunning floral display in May

autumn which persist through the winter. Violet-blue flowers in early spring. Any garden situation. Division when dormant.

✳ 🌿 G. × *lindavicum* (*argenteum* × *cinereum*)
Excellent rock plants similar in size and habit to G. *argenteum*. Leaves less silvery, flowers usually much more deeply coloured than in G. *argenteum*. Cuttings in spring.
　　'Alanah' (*argenteum* × *cinereum* var. *subcaulescens*). Silvery leaves and freely produced, reddish purple flowers.
　　'Apple Blossom' (= 'Jenny Bloom') (*argenteum* × *cinereum* var. *cinereum*, possibly backcrossed to G. *argenteum*). Silver-grey leaves and very pale pink, almost white, lightly veined petals. Exceptionally pretty.
　　'Lissadell' (G. *argenteum* × G. *cinereum* var. *subcaulescens*). Strongly veined, deep reddish purple flowers.

✳ G. 'Little Gem' (*oxonianum* × *traversii*)
A recent hybrid similar to the well-known 'Russell Prichard' but the leaves are flatter, and the flowers though slightly smaller are more intensely coloured – a bright reddish purple. May to October. Ground cover; border, large rock garden. Division.

G. *lucidum*
An annual species with rounded, glossy, rather succulent leaves on

Needing plenty of room in the border, the hybrid 'Nimbus' has starry flowers and finely divided leaves

red stems, and small pink flowers. The leaves colour well as they die away. Spring and summer. Self-seeding ground cover for the wild garden, even in dry shade.

*G. macrorrhizum

One of the most useful of all geraniums. It is easy to grow and propagate, and is drought resistant. It has evergreen, pleasantly scented leaves and flowers abundantly in early summer. The best ground-cover geranium, which also makes a good specimen plant.

  *'Album' (= var. album). Petals white, pink-stained at the base and the sepals and stamens dark pink. G. macrorrhizum 'Spessart' is identical though magenta-flowered plants have also been sold wrongly as 'Spessart'.

  'Bevan's Variety' (= 'Bevan'). Deep reddish purple flowers and deep red sepals.

  *'Czakor'. Similar to 'Bevan's Variety' but the flowers are slightly more strongly coloured.

  *'Ingwersen's Variety' (= 'Walter Ingwersen'). Pale pink flowers.

  'Ridsko'. Reddish purple flowers, shiny leaves and blackish exposed rhizomes.

  'Spessart' see 'Album'

  'Variegatum'. The leaves are brightly variegated in two shades of green, cream and grey. The flowers are reddish purple and growth is much weaker than in other forms.

40

SMALL FORMS

Three forms of wild origin have been described. These are only about half the size of typical *G. macrorrhizum*, have scarcely scented, thinner textured, less hairy, almost glossy leaves with larger spaces between the leaf divisions.

∗ **'Lohfelden'**. A low habit of growth. The flowers have very pale pink, almost white petals, veined deeper pink with orange anthers and red filaments.

∗ **'Pindus'**. Reddish purple flowers and an almost spherical shiny red calyx. The petals are broad and overlapping, and are red-stained at the base.

∗ **'Velebit'**. Reddish purple flowers held well above the mound of leaves. The petals are rather narrow with space between them and are colourless at the base. The calyx is reddish and hairy.

G. macrostylum
A small summer-dormant species. The leaves, growing in autumn and winter, are very deeply and finely cut and the delicate upward facing flowers, held well above the leaves, are pale purplish pink with a dark centre and veined petals. May. Proliferates by means of small tubers and is said to become a nuisance in rock gardens.

G. maculatum
Tall plants with handsome leaves, deeply split into five clearly separated divisions. Flowers pink to bluish purple, upward facing, borne in clusters on long stems well above the leaves. April to June. Border, woodland. Division; seed.

Var. *album*. Smaller, with masses of pure white flowers in spring.

∗ 🌿 *G. maderense*
The largest of all geraniums. A huge rosette of very large shiny leaves grows in autumn and winter and the flowers are borne in a massive inflorescence from early March to June. Flowers reddish purple with very dark centres; large numbers of purple glandular hairs on the flower stalks give the inflorescence an extra purplish cast. Best grown in the border of a greenhouse or in a very large pot. Young plants need frequent potting on to keep them in active growth or flowers will not be produced. Seed.

∗ *G. × magnificum*
(*G. ibericum* subsp. *ibericum* × *platypetalum*)
Probably the most commonly cultivated and widely available

geranium. It makes a truly magnificent display of large bluish purple flowers on large plants in May and into June, but flowering is not recurrent. Cut right back after flowering as the very large leaf mounds tend to smother adjacent plants. Border; wild/woodland garden; drought tolerant. Division.

G. malviflorum (= G. atlanticum [misapplied])
A tuberous summer-dormant species. The erect stems have deeply and freely divided leaves and the upward-facing flowers, borne in clusters are bluish purple and veined. Flowers best in a hot, dry situation. April to May. Rock garden; wild garden. Separation of tubers.

✳**G. 'Mavis Simpson'** (endressii or oxonianum × traversii)
(= G. × riversleaianum 'Mavis Simpson')
A trailing plant with grey-green leaves and flowers with pale purplish pink petals with fine dark purple veins. May to September. Ground cover; border; large rock garden. Division.

G. × monacense (phaeum × reflexum)
Very similar in appearance and garden value to G. phaeum. April to June. Ground cover; woodland. Division.
　　G. monacense nothovar. monacense (phaeum var. phaeum × reflexum). The flowers have reddish purple reflexed petals with a relatively large white basal zone.
　　'Muldoon'. The correct name for the cultivar sold for many years as G. punctatum, a name with no botanical or horticultural standing. A cultivar with characteristic heavy chocolate-brown blotching at the base of the divisions of the leaf lobes.
　　G. monacense nothovar. anglicum (phaeum var. lividum × reflexum). The flowers have pale reddish purple reflexed petals with a small white basal zone and a conspicuous bluish violet, strongly veined zone above.

G. nepalense
Sprawling habit and dark evergreen leaves which are purplish beneath and strikingly spotted maroon-brown above. It has small pale pink flowers in summer. Wild garden. Self seeding.

G. nervosum
Upright plants with rather sharply lobed leaf divisions and stems covered with sticky hairs. Flowers upward facing, borne well above the leaves, pink to reddish purple with veined petals. Recurrent from May onwards. Woodland/wild garden. Seed.

✱G. 'Nimbus' (*collinum* × *clarkei* 'Kashmir Purple')
A large spreading plant with finely and sharply divided leaves which are golden-tinged when young. Flowers bluish purple with a small pale centre, petals finely veined and relatively narrow with spaces between them giving the flowers a starry appearance. May to July. Border. Division.

✱G. nodosum
Glossy leaves in which the divisions are toothed but not lobed. Flowers erect, funnel shaped. May to September. Three colour forms have been named:
'Svelte Lilac'. Pale bluish purple flowers.
'Swish Purple'. Bluish purple flowers with a paler centre.
'Whiteleaf'. Bluish purple very pale-edged petals.

✱G. 'Nora Bremner'
(*rubifolium* × *wallichianum* 'Buxton's Variety')
Beautiful, large, soft violet-blue flowers are borne well above a mound of marbled leaves. Petals separate from each other traversed by fine veins and paler at the base giving the flowers a starry appearance with a large white centre. Midsummer to autumn. Shady border; woodland; in soil that does not dry out in summer. Careful division in spring.

Left: G. oreganum has large soft-textured flowers. The large plants need staking when grown in the border
Right: The flowers of G. sylvaticum 'Amy Doncaster' are among the bluest of all geraniums

G. oreganum

A large plant usually needing some support, with leaves similar to those of G. pratense. Flowers large, white-centred with reddish purple, rounded petals. May to June, recurrent to August. Border. Seed.

🍂 G. orientalitibeticum

Small plants with very strongly marbled leaves. Reddish purple flowers with a white centre in late May and June. Rock garden. Grows from chains of small tubers and can be invasive.

*G. x oxonianum (endressii x versicolor)

An important hybrid with many named cultivars. All have a strong constitution and are tolerant of a wide range of conditions and soils. They are also prolific in growth and easy to increase and are thus excellent ground cover plants. The mounds of new leaves in early spring are themselves an important part of the garden scene. The flowers are produced recurrently in good quantity from May to September but it is wise to cut the plants to the ground around midsummer, after the first main flush of flowers, when fresh leaf mounds will soon be produced followed by more flowers. Left to themselves, the old stems begin to sprawl, the fresh leaves rising up in the middle of the plant.

The size of the plants varies considerably as does the leaf marking though the leaves are always blotched with brown, to a greater or lesser degree, at the base of the leaf divisions. The flowers vary from palest pink to deep pink, sometimes tending towards salmon. In some cultivars, the flowers change colour as they age, this producing an attractive speckled effect. It is almost invariably stated that the flowers fade, but the reverse is true, the youngest flowers always being the palest. Border; woodland/wild garden. Division.

Since this hybrid is fertile and can intercross or backcross to either of the parents, many cultivars have been named (some would say far too many!) and it is likely that even more will appear.

*'A. T. Johnson'. Silvery pink flowers, darkening somewhat with age. Leaves pale green.

*'Claridge Druce'. Plants large with a hoary appearance,

G. orientalitibeticum has the most strongly marbled leaves of all the species presently in cultivation and is easy to grow in the rock garden or the front of a sunny border

flowers correspondingly large, over $1\frac{1}{2}$ in. (4 cm) in diameter, reddish purple with a strong network of dark veins.

'Hollywood'. Similar to 'Claridge Druce' with smaller and greener (not hoary) leaves. Flowers large, up to $1\frac{1}{2}$ in. (4 cm) in diameter with broad overlapping petals; these have a prominent network of purple veins on a pale reddish pink ground.

'Lady Moore' (= 'Lady Moore's Variety'). Similar to 'Claridge Druce' with large bluish green leaves with brown blotches at the bases of the divisions. Flowers reddish purple with darker veins, but the veining is not as prominent as in 'Hollywood' and 'Claridge Druce'.

*'Miriam Rundle' (*G. oxonianum* 'Thurstonianum' x *G. oxonianum* 'Claridge Druce'). Smaller and less vigorous than other cultivars. Flowers deep purplish red and prominently veined.

'Old Rose'. Slightly shorter than most other cultivars with a remarkable variation in flower colour. The youngest flowers are mid reddish purple while the older flowers are much darker. The petals are prominently veined.

*'Phoebe Noble'. Strong purplish red flowers. The darkest cultivar.

*'Rebecca Moss'. Very pale pink flowers, without darker veins. One of the palest pink cultivars.

*'Rose Clair'. An old cultivar with deep pink flowers.

*'Rosenlicht' (= *G. endressii* 'Rosenlicht'). The flowers are strong purplish pink.

'Sherwood'. Similar to 'Thurstonianum' but has longer and narrower petals which are pale pink.

'Southcombe Star'. Flowers with narrow strap-shaped petals which are reddish purple in colour with a network of darker veins. The stamens are often petaloid (resembling petals).

'Southcombe Double'. A relatively small cultivar. Flowers salmon-pink. The stamens are usually petaloid producing double flowers which are sometimes even pom-pon-like. Early and late in the season plants may produce mainly or only normal single flowers.

'Thurstonianum'. Plants large, the flowers with very narrow, deep reddish purple petals, and petaloid stamens. Many clones are included under this name, all of which seem to originate as seedlings from 'Claridge Druce'.

*'Wageningen'. Bright salmon-pink flowers.

*'Walter's Gift'. Very heavy chocolate-brown blotched leaves, particularly early in the season. Flowers with pale pink petals strongly veined reddish purple.

*'**Wargrave Pink**' (= *endressii* 'Wargrave Pink'). Plants tall, flowers light salmon-pink. One of the classic border geraniums.

*'**Winscombe**'. Shorter than most other cultivars. Remarkable for the change in flower colour from very pale pink, almost white, in the youngest flowers to purplish pink and finally to purplish red as the flowers go over.

G. 'Pagoda' (*sinense* × *yunnanense*)

Tall plants with rather lax and wiry leafy stems needing some support. The leaves are marbled and the petals of the nodding flowers lie flat but curl back slightly as they age. They are of a remarkable and unique colour for *Geranium*, dark reddish purple with a velvety texture which emphasises the richness of the colouring. Part shade in soil that does not dry out in summer. Midsummer to September. Division.

G. palmatum (= *anemonifolium*)

Huge evergreen rosettes of very large leaves and a tall inflorescence of pale reddish purple flowers with a dark centre. Flower stalks covered in purple glandular hairs as in *G. maderense*. Hardy in the south of England in normal winters. May to August. Border. Seed.

G. palustre

Rounded cushions of shiny coarsely lobed leaves. Flowers bright reddish purple. June to September. Wild/woodland garden. Division; seed.

'**Plus**'. Larger flowers borne on taller plants. Possibly a hybrid with *G. sylvaticum*.

*G. 'Patricia' (endressii × psilostemon)

Tall plants with very large handsome leaves and large bright reddish purple, dark-centred flowers. June to late September. An outstanding new hybrid for the border. Division.

G. peloponnesiacum

A summer-dormant species with bluish purple flowers on tall stems in April and May. Of similar garden value to *G. libani*. Division when dormant.

*G. phaeum

Mounds of more or less evergreen leaves. The long, leafy, sparsely-branched flowering stems are produced in spring and early

Left: A hybrid between G. *sinense* and G. *yunnanense*, 'Pagoda' has dark velvety flowers of a colour unique among geraniums
Right: G. *sinense*, a parent of 'Pagoda', has almost black velvety petals

summer. The horizontally held nodding flowers are up to 1 in. (2.5 cm) in diameter and vary from reddish purple to bluish purple. The petals are rather ruffled round the edge. A woodland ground cover species *par excellence*, its demure beauty, charming in any spring display. Division.

G. *phaeum* var. *phaeum*. The petals are sharply pointed and different forms vary in colour from pale shades of bluish purple and pink, through reddish purple, bluish purple to very dark purple, nearly black. They have a prominent white zone at the base.

'Album'. Pure white flowers.

'Calligrapher'. The petals have a short sharp tip and the edges are strongly ruffled. The edge and base of each petal is bluish purple but the central part is very pale and the deep violet veins extending across this region are, therefore, particularly prominent. The leaves are prominently blotched with purplish brown in the notches.

'Langthorn's Blue'. Bluish purple flowers with pale centred petals.

'Lily Lovell'. Particularly large bluish purple flowers with reflexed petals.

'Mourning Widow'. Flowers very dark purple, almost black.

'Rose Madder'. The brownish pink of the flowers is a unique colour among geraniums.

🦋 **'Samobor'.** Leaves heavily zoned with chocolate brown. Worth growing for its foliage alone.

🦋 **'Variegatum'.** Leaves very irregularly edged in white, with

48

maroon blotches in the white areas, particularly at the base of the divisions.

G. phaeum var. lividum. The petals are rounded and pale bluish purple in the forms commonly in cultivation. They have a white base, smaller than that in var. *phaeum*, above which is a bluish halo composed of short violet veins; there is usually another whitish halo above this.

'Joan Baker'. A tall cultivar, with flowers over 1 in. (2.5 cm) in diameter, pale reddish purple in colour with a deeper halo near the centre.

'Majus'. Inflorescences tall, up to 33 in. (83 cm) with flowers up to 1¼ in. (3 cm) across.

*G. 'Philippe Vapelle' (*platypetalum* × *renardii*)
Blue-grey softly-hairy leaves are intermediate in shape between those of the parents with a textured surface as in *G. renardii*. The flowers are bluish purple with prominently veined and deeply notched petals. June to July. Border. Division.

G. platyanthum (= *eriostemon*)
A tall, sturdy, hairy plant with large pale green shallow-lobed leaves and mid-bluish purple flowers in umbel-like clusters in May and June. Wild/woodland garden. Seed.

Forma *albiflorum* has white flowers with yellow anthers; the plants are smaller than the typical form.

G. platypetalum
A noticeably hairy plant with similar but less complexly divided leaves than its relatives *G. ibericum* and *G.* × *magnificum*. The sombre bluish purple flowers are recurrent from May onwards. Border; wild/woodland garden. Division.

G. pogonanthum
Deeply and sharply cut, strongly marbled leaves and exquisite nodding flowers with recurved petals. Flowers are pale pink with a white centre and a strongly contrasting central column of purplish red stamen filaments. July to September. Part shade with plenty of summer moisture. Seed or division.

G. potentilloides
A low spreading plant with small leaves and small white flowers in summer. Rock garden. Seed.

G. polyanthes
Rather small fleshy leaves with a rounded outline and reddish purple, funnel-shaped flowers in July. The leaves do not appear until late spring. Woodland garden. Seed.

*****G. pratense** Meadow cranesbill
 G. pratense subsp. pratense. The most important large geranium for the garden, almost every variation being worth cultivating. The flowers are produced in June and July on tall branching stems above a large mound of handsome leaves. Plants should be given some support when grown in the border. Many cultivars have been named and only a selection of the most distinct forms is listed. The cultivars readily hybridise and are best propagated by division in spring.
 'Bicolor' see 'Striatum'.
 *****'Galactic'.** Not only are the flowers pure white, but the whole plant lacks any red (anthocyanin) pigment.
 'Kashmir Purple' see G. clarkei 'Kashmir Purple'.
 'Kashmir White' see G. clarkei 'Kashmir White'.
 'Lilacina'. Pale violet-blue flowers.
 *****'Mrs Kendall Clark'.** Flowers violet-blue with a network of prominent white veins.
 'Plenum Album'. Frilly double white flowers with a green centre, the small innermost petals stained reddish purple and veined with the same colour. Temperamental in cultivation, tending to die in winter.
 'Plenum Caeruleum'. Rather loosely double, violet-blue flowers of similar form to those of 'Plenum Album'. The smaller innermost petals tinged purplish red.
 'Plenum Violaceum'. Deep bluish purple flowers, very double, rose-like. The smaller innermost petals paler.
 *****'Rose Queen'** (= roseum). Flowers with very pale pink, nearly white petals. The dense network of pinkish purple veins makes the overall flower colour appear pink. The anthers are orange which emphasises the flower colour.
 *****'Silver Queen'.** Flowers of palest violet-blue with conspicuous black anthers.
 *****'Striatum'** (= 'Bicolor'). One of the most easily recognisable of all geranium cultivars. The petals are white, irregularly spotted and streaked with violet-blue so that every petal and flower is different. Different petals in the same flower may be almost all-white or all-blue, or half-white and half-blue, or streaked or spotted, or both. The markings vary during the season.

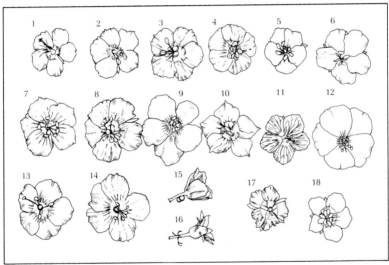

Geranium phaeum and relatives

1 *phaeum* 'Mourning Widow' **2–6** *phaeum*; unnamed colour forms
7 *phaeum* 'Langthorn's Blue' **8** *phaeum* 'Lily Lovell'
9 *phaeum* var. *lividum* 'Joan Baker' **10** *phaeum* 'Calligrapher'
11 *phaeum* 'Rose Madder' **12** *phaeum* 'Album' **13** *phaeum* var. *lividum*
14 *phaeum* var. *lividum* 'Majus' **15–16** two colour forms of *G. reflexum*
17 × *monacense* **18** × *monacense* nothovar. *anglicum*

Forma *albiflorum*. The name for all white-flowered plants not otherwise distinguished by a cultivar name.

Subsp. *stewartianum* var. *stewartianum*. The habit of the plant is similar to that in subsp. *pratense* though somewhat less leafy. The flowers are 1½ in. (4 cm) in diameter typically with bluish purple flowers. The flowers are produced much earlier than in subsp. *pratense*, in April and May, and then recurrently.

✳'**Elizabeth Yeo'**. A clone with mid-purplish pink flowers. The best tall early flowering border geranium.

G. procurrens

Long trailing and scrambling leafy stems which readily root at the leaf joints. The flowers have dusky bluish purple petals with a black zone at the base and prominent black veins. The centre of the flower is thus very dark and the effect is enhanced by the black stamen filaments. July to September. Ground cover; border; wild garden.

✳G. psilostemon

A splendid plant, tall, with large leaves and bright reddish purple flowers with a black centre and black veins. The vibrant flower colour is sometimes considered difficult to place, but it associates

Left: 'Philippe Vapelle' is a summer-flowering hybrid with leaves and flowers intermediate in character between those of its parents G. *platypetalum* and G. *renardii*

Right: G. *pratense* 'Mrs Kendall Clark' is one of the best known and most easily recognisable cultivars of the meadow cranesbill

well with other reds and purples and pastel blues and silvers. One of the best border geraniums. June to July. Seed; division.

  ∗'Bressingham Flair'. Paler pinker flowers than the species.

G. pulchrum

A hardy South African species, the sprawling stems becoming woody at the base to make a spreading mound of fingered evergreen leaves, grey-green above, silvery and silky beneath. Flowers large, bluish purple, from July to September. Border. Seed; cuttings.

G. pylzowianum

A small plant with small, deeply divided fan-shaped leaves. Flowers reddish purple in May and June. Grows from small tubers and may become invasive in rock gardens.

G. pyrenaicum

A rather coarse mounding plant with rounded evergreen leaves and small flowers. Flowering recurrent from May onwards. The typical form has pale bluish purple flowers. Vigorous and very free-seeding, and can become a weed.

  ∗'Bill Wallis'. Deep bluish purple flowers, and is smaller than the typical form.

  Forma albiflorum. Flowers white.

G. 'Rebecca'

(*cinereum* subsp. *subcaulescens* × *traversii* var. *elegans*)
A rock plant with golden green leaves when young. Purplish pink flowers. May to July. Has not achieved initial promise.

G. rectum

An erect plant with sparsely leafy stems and reddish purple, funnel-shaped flowers from May to September. Wild garden. Division; seed.

G. reflexum

Similar to G. phaeum but the flowers have narrower petals which are strongly reflexed so the flowers are only about ⅜ in. (10 mm) across. The petals are pink, white at the base and with a bluish band where they bend backwards. April to June. Woodland. Division.

G. regelii

Related to, and very much like a small form of G. pratense. Large pale violet-blue flowers in May and recurrent. Rock garden. Division; seed.

*G. renardii

'Walter Ingwersen'. The well-known form with grey-green, lobed leaves which have a finely wrinkled sage-like texture. Flowers large, palest bluish purple with dark veins. One of the most easily recognisable of all geraniums both in flower and in leaf. May. Rock garden, border. Division in spring.

'Whiteknights'. Plants are looser in habit with longer flower stalks. Flowers mid bluish purple prominently veined less freely produced.

G. rivulare

Erect plants with deeply divided and finely cut leaves. Clusters of small funnel-shaped flowers with white petals and fine violet veins. May to June. Wild/woodland garden. Seed.

G. robertianum Herb Robert

The familiar British native reddish purple flowered annual garden weed. Grows all winter if allowed to do so and then flowers in spring and summer. The white-flowered form G. robertianum 'Album' is attractive in informal situations but is also a persistent seeder. The only tolerable cultivar for the average garden is 'Celtic White' which is both dwarf and compact with bright green leaves and small pure white flowers.

G. richardsonii

Mounds of glossy, deeply divided leaves and white flowers produced in April to May, and recurrently to September. Rock garden; wild garden. Seed.

G. x riversleaianum see G. 'Russell Prichard' and G. 'Mavis Simpson'

G. robustum

A hardy South African species, sprawling or scrambling leafy stems, woody at base. Evergreen, fingered leaves are greyish green above, silvery beneath. Flowers bluish purple with a white centre, produced recurrently from May onwards. Border. Seed; cuttings.

G. rubescens

Slightly tender biennial with a large over-wintering rosette of leaves with beetroot red leaf stalks. The reddish purple flowers are recurrent from early summer. It resembles a giant *G. robertianum*, but self-seeds only mildly. Sheltered border. Seed.

G. *rubifolium*
Similar to a large form of its close relative *G. kishtvariense*; the two species readily hybridise. Leaves with only a small number of broad divisions and large upward-facing, reddish purple flowers with a pale centre on loose leafy stems. Midsummer onwards. Shady border or woodland. Seed.

G. 'Russell Prichard' (*endressii* or *oxonianum* × *traversii*)
(= *G.* × *riversleaianum* 'Russell Prichard')
A trailing plant with grey-green hairy leaves spreading to about 3 ft (90 cm) in one season. Flowers reddish purple. Well known for its very long period of flowering, from May to October. Ground cover, border, large rock garden. Division.

G. *sanguineum* Bloody cranesbill
Popular and easy to grow species with spreading, eventually

Hybrid geraniums and their parents. From left to right, above: *ibericum*, *platypetalum*, *renardii*; below: × *magnificum* (*ibericum* × *platypetalum*), 'Philippe Vapelle' (*platypetalum* × *renardii*), *renardii* 'Whiteknights'

Some cultivars of G. *sanguinieum*. From left to right, above: 'Nyewood', 'Cedric Morris', 'Elsbeth', typical form; below: 'Shepherd's Warning' var. *striatum*, 'Splendens' var. *striatum*, 'Album'

mounding leafy stems. Leaves small, deeply and narrowly divided. Flowers large relative to the size of the plant, borne freely between May and August. Very variable in size and flower colour, and a large and ever-increasing number of cultivars has been named. Front of border; rock garden. Stem and rhizome cuttings.

✳ **'Album'**. Pristine white flowers on relatively tall plants.

✳ **'Ankum's Pride'**. Compact plants with bright pink flowers and darker veins.

'Cedric Morris'. Plants up to 2 ft (60 cm) tall with large reddish purple flowers almost 2 in. (5 cm) in diameter.

✳ **'Elsbeth'**. Similar to 'Cedric Morris' but with hairy leaves and more vividly coloured flowers.

✳ **'Glenluce'**. Plants tall, spreading, with dark green leaves covered with silky hairs. Pale reddish purple flowers with a fine network of darker veins.

✳ **'Holden'**. Spreading habit, small leaves and bright pink flowers.

✳ **'Jubilee Pink'**. Plants compact, flowers bright purplish pink.

'Max Frei'. Plants compact, flowers bright reddish purple.

'Minutum'. Plants only about 2 in. (5 cm) tall with very small leaves but with normal sized, reddish purple flowers.

'Nyewood'. Plants compact with small leaves but eventually reaching 18 in. (45 cm) tall. Flowers reddish purple.

'Plenum'. Plants relatively small, flowers purplish red with frilled "overlarge" petals, sometimes with extra petals, but never fully double.

✳**'Shepherd's Warning'.** Similar to 'Jubilee Pink' but more compact and with deeper pink flowers.

var. _lancastriense_ see _G. sanguineum_ var. _striatum_.

✳**_G. sanguineum_ var. _striatum_** (= _G. sanguineum_ var. _lancastriense_; = _G. sanguineum_ var. _prostratum_, in part). A well-known relatively large variety with pale pink petals with darker pink veins. Different clones vary in habit and leaf colour.

'Splendens'. Petals distinctly wrinkled and more strongly veined than var. _striatum_ so they appear slightly darker.

G. schlechteri
A hardy South African species with vigorous scrambling growth and small white or pink flowers from July onwards. Wild garden, but self-seeds prolifically and can become a pest.

G. 'Sea Fire'
(_sessiliflorum_ subsp. _novaezelandiae_ 'Nigricans' × _oxonianum_)
Low spreading, eventually mounding growth with small brownish evergreen leaves and small bright purplish red flowers with a pale centre. A neat plant flowering from May to September. Rock garden. Division; cuttings.

G. 'Sea Pink'
(_sessiliflorum_ subsp. _novaezelandiae_ 'Nigricans' × _oxonianum_)
Similar to 'Sea Fire' but with dark green leaves and pink flowers.

G. 'Sea Spray'
(_traversii_ var. _elegans_ × _sessiliflorum_ subsp. _novaezelandiae_ 'Nigricans')
Leafy flowering stems spread to about 4 ft (1.2 m) from a mound of bronzy green leaves. The green-throated flowers vary from very pale pink, almost white, to pale pink. June to September. Ground cover; border. Division; cuttings.

G. sessiliflorum subsp. novaezelandiae
A dwarf plant with small green leaves and tiny white flowers borne recurrently. Little garden value. Seed.

'Nigricans'. Plants larger than the type with dark bronzy leaves. Rock garden. Seed.

'Porter's Pass'. The largest form presently in cultivation, reaching about 6 in. (15 cm) tall. Very distinct beetroot red leaves. Seed.

G. shikokianum
A modest, beautiful geranium, sharply cut leaves usually marbled yellow-green above, glossy beneath. Flowers pale reddish purple with a large white centre, petals finely veined. July to September. Woodland, in soil that does not dry out in summer. Seed.

G. sinense
Plants tall, flowers nodding with strongly swept-back petals which are very dark reddish purple, almost black, with a velvety texture. The petals are paler at the base giving the flower a paler centre and the column of reddish purple stamens forms a distinct point. Leaves glossy, rich green and faintly marbled. Woodland garden in a place where the flowers can be closely inspected. Seed; division in spring.

G. soboliferum
Compact mounds of very finely and sharply cut leaves and flat reddish purple flowers. Inferior clones have rather wrinkled self-coloured petals while the most desirable have pale-tipped petals giving an unusual two-tone appearance. July to September. Wild/woodland garden. Seed.

*G. 'Spinners' (pratense × ?)
A magnificent hybrid forming large mounds of deeply cut leaves. Flowers rich bluish purple from May to July. 'Spinners' has a rather complex history and has been confused with G. clarkei 'Kashmir Purple' and wrongly called G. bergianum, a name formerly applied to 'Kashmir Purple'. Border. Division.

G. 'Stanhoe'
(sessiliflorum subsp. novaezelandiae × traversii var. elegans)
A central mound of green leaves similar in shape to those of G. traversii and much-branched, small leaved trailing flowering stems. Flowers white or white flushed pink. June to September. Rock garden. Division.

G. striatum see G. versicolor

G. swatense
Mounds of marbled leaves and flat reddish purple flowers with

pale centres produced continuously from June onwards. A valuable recent introduction. Seems to dislike winter wet. Rock garden; border. Seed.

G. sylvaticum Wood cranesbill

An important species for the woodland garden, the best cultivars also being suitable for beds and borders. Erect plants with deeply and finely divided leaves and sprays of bluish purple, white-centred flowers in the typical form. Relatively late into leaf. Division.

∗ **'Album'**. Pure white flowers and pale green leaves.

∗ **'Amy Doncaster'**. Violet-blue flowers with a white centre which are slightly smaller than in other varieties.

'Angulatum'. Larger than usual flowers with pale purplish pink prominently veined petals.

∗ **'Baker's Pink'**. Very pale pink flowers on plants up to 4 ft (1.2 m) tall.

'Birch Lilac'. Mid-bluish purple flowers.

∗ **'Mayflower'**. Bluish purple flowers with a small white centre. Slightly bluer than 'Birch Lilac'.

G. shikokianum produces its charming white-centred flowers in small numbers in late summer; it grows best in rich woodland soil

'**Silva**'. Bluish purple flowers with a white eye, larger and flatter than in the typical form. Less blue than 'Birch Lilac'.

subsp. *caeruleatum* see G. *caeruleatum*

Var. *wanneri*. Pale pink almost white petals which are beautifully veined with bright purplish pink. Less vigorous and lower growing than other forms.

*G. traversii var. elegans

A mound of grey, hairy, rounded leaves and spreading leafy flowering stems bearing purplish pink, firm-textured, finely veined flowers. June onwards. Border; rock garden. Seed; cuttings.

G. thunbergii

A vigorous sprawling plant with evergreen, light green leaves which are strongly blotched with brownish purple. Flowers small, white to deep reddish purple. August to October. Good ground cover for the wild garden, even in dry shade. Seed.

G. tuberosum

Summer-dormant, producing very finely divided leaves in early spring and abundant bluish purple flowers with darker veins in May. A variable species. Rock garden; border. Separation of tubers.

G. versicolor (= G. striatum)

Pale green evergreen leaves with chocolate-brown blotches and white funnel-shaped flowers beautifully net-veined with reddish purple. May to October. Remarkable flowers but rather sprawling habit and best in the wild/woodland garden. Division; seed.

'**Snow White**'. Pure white flowers lacking coloured veins. It has a more upright habit of growth than the species. Lovely in white and green colour schemes.

*G. viscosissimum

Large handsome leaves and upright flower stems covered with sticky hairs. These bear clusters of rather pale, reddish purple, finely veined flowers with a pale centre. Recurrent from April to August. Wild/woodland garden. Seed.

G. wallichianum

Trailing leafy stems, eventually mounding. Leaves shallowly lobed, marbled on the upper surface. Flowers variable in colour, produced from midsummer onwards. Border; woodland. Seed.

Although not very hardy, *G. traversii* var. *elegans* is a popular geranium which may be easily and quickly grown from seed

---

∗**'Buxton's Variety'** (= 'Buxton's Blue'). Large, saucer-shaped, violet-blue, white-centred flowers. One of the best late-flowering perennials.

∗**'Syabru'**. Bright reddish purple flowers, with a sheen to the petals. Said to be stronger growing and longer flowering than 'Buxton's Variety'.

✥ G. wlassovianum
Dense mounds of shallowly but sharply divided leaves and dark purple flowers from June to September. The young leaves are the colour of young oak leaves and the mature leaves are tinged purple-brown. Border; woodland. Seed; division.

G. yesoense
Bushy plants with small deeply cut leaves and white or very pale bluish purple dark-veined flowers from June to August. A modest plant for the wild/woodland garden or rock garden. Seed.

G. yunnanense
Rather loose mounds of marbled leaves and pink, bowl-shaped nodding flowers. Dislikes hot dry weather. Shady rock garden; woodland. Seed.

Index

Page numbers in **bold** refer to illustrations